– Peter Bergson –
The Jewish Lobbyist Who Advocated To Save Jews During the Holocaust

by Rabbi Dov Peretz Elkins
Winner of the National Jewish Book Award

Mazo Publishers

Peter Bergson – The Jewish Lobbyist Who Advocated To Save Jews During the Holocaust

ISBN 978-1-956381-22-1

Contact The Author
RabbiElkins@gmail.com

Mazo Publishers
Chaim Mazo, Publisher
Website: www.mazopublishers.com
Email: mazopublishers@gmail.com

David and Audrey Egger

dedicate this book

*in memory of David's father, Henry Egger's extended family
in The Netherlands, all of whom perished in the Holocaust*

In Memory of our Wonderful Grandparents

~ Rose and Azriel Eisenberg ~

Bryna and Joshua Landes

Contents

The Author

Dov Peretz Elkins is a nationally known lecturer, educator, workshop leader, author, and book critic. He is a popular speaker on the Jewish circuit.

Rabbi Elkins is a recipient of the National Jewish Book Award, and the author of over 56 books. His *Chicken Soup For The Jewish Soul* was on *The New York Times* bestseller list.

His most recent books are: *The Friendship That Shaped Jewish History* (Mazo Publishers), *Bialik: Israel's National Poet* (Mazo Publishers), *The Power of Human Speech* (Mazo Publishers), *FATE* (Mazo Publishers), *Jewish Ethical Wisdom From Pirkei Avot* (Mazo Publishers), *To Climb The Rungs – Memoirs of a Rabbi* (Mazo Publishers), *Jewish Stories from Heaven and Earth: Inspiring Tales to Nourish the Heart and Soul, Tales of the Righteous, Simple Actions for Jews to Help Green the Planet, Heart and Scroll: Inspiring Stories from the Masters* (Mazo Publishers), *In the Spirit: Insights for Spiritual Renewal in the 21st Century, For Those Left Behind: A Jewish Anthology of Comfort and Healing* (Mazo Publishers) and *A Treasury of Thoughts on Israel and Zionism* (Mazo Publishers).

Among Rabbi Elkins' other books are *Rosh Hashanah Readings: Inspiration, Information and Contemplation, Yom Kippur Readings,* and *The Wisdom of Judaism: An Introduction to the Values of the Talmud.* See other books by Dov Peretz Elkins at www.jewishgrowth.org.

Rabbi Elkins served in several outstanding congregations in Rochester, NY, Cleveland, OH, and in Princeton, NJ, before retirement. He earned a doctorate in pastoral counseling in Rochester, NY.

Dr. Elkins lives in Jerusalem with his wife, Maxine (Miryam). They have six children and twelve grandchildren.

Acknowledgments

I am very grateful to my dear friend and colleague, Rabbi Stephen Chaim Listfield, for his careful reading of the entire manuscript.

Deep appreciation to my good friends, David Egger and Joshua Landes, who frequently support my literary efforts.

Thanks, as always, to my publisher, Chaim Mazo, for his talented, skillful and artistic handling of several of my books.

Deep appreciation to my loving wife, Miryam, for sharing my goals in spreading Jewish knowledge to others.

Dov Peretz Elkins
Tu BiShvat, 5782
Jerusalem, Israel
The Seventy-fourth year of the State of Israel
The Fifty-fifth year of the Unification of Jerusalem

Comments on Rabbi Elkins' Books

Rabbi Dov Peretz Elkins tells the heroic story of Peter Bergson (born Hillel Kook) who understood before most Nazi Germany's genocidal intentions and devoted great efforts to mobilize the United States, in particular, to save European Jewry. Written in a manner accessible to young people and also of great interest to adults, Elkins reminds us that Germany's intentions were no secret, that American Jewry did not do enough to help, and that one man can make an extraordinary difference. Especially in light of the resigned cynicism that often meets claims of human rights violations today, the story of Peter Bergson is important to retell.

Dr. Jeffrey Herbst, President, American Jewish University.

Dov Peretz Elkins has written an important book for young people. It is the heartbreaking story of a neglected Jewish hero, Peter Bergson (born Hillel Kook), and his desperate efforts to rally the United States government and people to make a significant attempt to save Jews from the Nazi "Final Solution" exterminations program which engulfed European Jewry.

The apathy of President Franklin D. Roosevelt and the Administration, and unwillingness to act is vividly portrayed. The shocking indifference of mainstream American Jewish organizations and the callous policies of not rocking the boat pursued by Rabbi Stephen Wise are exposed. The spiteful attacks on Bergson and his various organizations and their allies by do-nothing organizations are ever more devastating to read.

Elkins describes the one success of all the rescue efforts – the appointment of a War Refugee Board which saved as many as 200,000 Jewish lives. One could argue that Elkins gives all the credit to Bergson and that Secretary of Treasury Morgenthau and his team's role is downplayed. But this would be nitpicking. All in all, this book is an important moral contribution. It pays a long overdue debt to Peter Bergson, to history and to memory. Tragically, it makes clear that human failures enabled the Nazis to operate with little resistance from America (as from the Allies and bystanders in Europe.) This book deserves a wide readership.

Rabbi Irving (Yitz) Greenberg.
Dr. Greenberg served as Executive Director of the President's Commission on the Holocaust, which recommended the creation of the U.S. Holocaust Memorial Museum, and later as chairman of USHMM (2000-2002).

Peter Bergson (Hillel Kook) was among the first Jews in America to internalize the idea that the Germans were implementing the Final Solution to the Jewish Problem, murdering Jewish men, women and children throughout German-occupied Europe. He understood that this was not a time for business as usual and he raised a ruckus, pulling out all the stops to call attention to the plight of the Jews and to plead for rescue. He organized, he publicized, he cajoled, he yelled, he planned, and he tried idea after idea.

History has vindicated his radicalism, his activism, and his boldness. Dov Peretz Elkins has made an important contribution in bringing Bergson to life, portraying him for a new generation, where he can become a model, an inspiration.

Dr. Michael Berenbaum, Professor of Jewish Studies
Director of Sigi Ziering Institute:
Exploring the Ethical and Religious Implications of the Holocaust.
American Jewish University, Los Angeles, CA

Few friendships in all of American Jewish history have been as impactful for Jews as the one between Eddie Jacobson and Harry S. Truman. Dov Peretz Elkins ably recounts the story of that friendship and what it meant for the emerging State of Israel. An inspiring story.

Jonathan D. Sarna, University Professor and Joseph H. & Belle R. Braun Professor of American Jewish History, Brandeis University

Dov Peretz Elkins is one of the most spiritual people I know. His creative work in education and nourishing human beings is known throughout the world. He has made another useful contribution through this marvelous collection of spiritual quotations. His work continues to be chicken soup for my soul.

Jack Canfield, co-author, Chicken Soup For the Soul

"So, four rabbis walk into... a deli..." Sounds like the beginning of a joke, but fortunately for us, it is actually the set up for a compelling peek behind the closed door of the rabbi's study. These thoughtful colleagues bring all sorts of fascinating questions to discuss with each other as they grapple with the key Jewish questions of our time: Jewish practice, intermarriage, fostering welcoming and inclusive communities, The rabbis may be fictional, but the brilliant Rabbi Dov Peretz Elkins is sharing truths stranger and more meaningful than fiction. If you've ever wondered how rabbis make decisions, grab this book. You'll find it hard to put down!

Dr. Ron Wolfson, Fingerhut Prof. of Education, American Jewish Univ.

Rabbi Elkins has written an engaging book, involving discussions among four rabbis of different religious movements. Through these conversations, readers gain insight into major – and minor – issues in Judaism. It's an opportunity for readers to "eavesdrop" on rabbis who are on the front lines of Jewish life...to agree or disagree with them, to engage in their discussions.

Rabbi Marc D. Angel is Founder and Director of the Institute for Jewish Ideas and Ideals and author of many books.

At a tumultuous moment in our society, Jews are searching for ways to understand and address the many controversies in our faith and society that threaten to overwhelm us. Many feel unequipped to answer these questions because they do not have formal religious training. Dov Peretz Elkins, by allowing us to be the proverbial "fly on the wall" during conversations between four rabbis, enriches, educates and entertains us. At the same time, he shows the very human side of our faith's leaders.

Professor Jeffrey Herbst, President, American Jewish University

This is the kind of book in which you say to yourself after reading it, "Why did it take so long for someone to think of doing this?" [*Jewish Ethical Wisdom From Pirkei Avot*] Pirkei Avot (Ethics of the Fathers) has had centuries of commentaries, but now, for the first time, multiple commentaries on many of its passages are arranged according to topic. This will make it much more user friendly, just as the Mishnah made Jewish law more accessible by organizing it by topic. Furthermore, the wealth of commentaries that Rabbi Elkins has amassed on each topic, including classical, medieval, and modern voices, makes what the original Mishnah says all the more relevant and meaningful. We all should be grateful to Rabbi Elkins for writing this book.

Elliot Dorff, Rabbi, Ph.D., Rector and Distinguished Service Professor of Philosophy, American Jewish University

Four Rabbis at Lunch is a marvelous discussion sprinkled with seriousness, humor and a great amount of important information about what rabbis have to deal with whatever their denomination and struggles. Much to learn from, to have a good laugh, and think what Judaism is all about and why it is of crucial importance. The most important message of this book is that rabbis with very different ideas about Judaism can sit together, listen to each other and have an actual discussion. A hopeful sign!

Rabbi Dr. Nathan Lopes Cardozo, Jerusalem

My family reads these stories out loud to each other. We laugh. We cry. A family that eats chicken soup together will remain culinary Jews. A family that reads *Chicken Soup for the Jewish Soul* together will remain part of an enduring tradition that has transformed the world with its humor, passion and generosity of spirit.

Alan M. Dershowitz, Felix Frankfurter Professor Emeritus of Law, Harvard University Law School.

In the Spirit is a lovely and accessible compendium of Jewish virtues that draws on our traditions of wisdom from the Bible to modern writers. Rabbi Elkins' own stories and comments make this book a valuable guide that can accompany the reader on many occasions.

David Ariel, PhD, former President of the Oxford Centre for Hebrew and Jewish Studies at the University of Oxford

If your curiosity ever tempted you to eavesdrop on your Rabbi's conversation with his colleagues in order to overhear their thoughts on some of the most significant and relevant topics of Judaism for today, this is the book you must acquire and read.

Professor Shalom Paul, former Chair, Dept. of Bible, the Hebrew University, Jerusalem

Rabbi Dov Peretz Elkins is a leading spiritual figure in our time, and all his writings are of high quality.

Rabbi Zalman Schachter-Shalomi, author of Davening: A Guide to Meaningful Jewish Prayer

Since the 60s, I have cherished the books by Rabbi Elkins. He is generous and brave, traditional and cutting edge. He is a great teacher because he is a great student. Rabbi Elkins is a gifted Rabbi and teacher and writer. I always purchase his new books sight unseen, and I am always grateful for what he has written.

Arthur Kurzweil, Author of On the Road with Rabbi Steinsaltz and From Generation
to Generation: How to Trace Your Jewish Genealogy

Based on his lifetime of experience in the Conservative rabbinate, Dov Peretz Elkins invites readers to eavesdrop as four fictional rabbis – Conservative, Orthodox and Reform – gather weekly to converse and schmooze. Major issues that rabbis face in their work – everything from intermarriage and Israel to circumcision and sex – fill out these conversations, which are punctuated by learning, humor and practical wisdom.

Jonathan D. Sarna, University Professor and Joseph H. & Belle R. Braun Professor
of American Jewish History, Brandeis University

Through the lunch-table conversation of four imaginary rabbis, *Four Rabbis at Lunch* offers the reader an original perspective on the Jewish community and Jewish religious leadership in our time by a master rabbi drawing on his decades of experience in the Jewish community. The book's unprecedented fictional format provides the layman with a witty, anecdotal, and memorable entree into the complex, sometimes contradictory intellectual, moral, and social currents that lie behind the polished words of the preacher and the wise counsel of the pastor.

Raymond Scheindlin, Professor Emeritus, Jewish Theological Seminary

Imagining, visualization, and meditation have been part of Jewish prayer and life for the longest time. In the

Talmud we read that the early hasidim would spend an hour before prayer in order to direct their minds to God. In his book on guided imagery, Dov Peretz Elkins helps the Jewish community recapture this grand tradition and practice. This guidebook will assist all who dare experience a new way of Jewish growth and development.

Rabbi Samuel K. Joseph, Ph.D., Professor of Jewish Education, Hebrew Union College – Jewish Institute of Religion

A most creative application of guided imagery techniques to Jewish education. If my Hebrew school teachers had used these tools to involve me personally and emotionally in my Jewish heritage, I would not have had to reach my thirties before coming to accept and prize my Jewishness. These activities are interesting, enjoyable, practical and useful with young people and adults.

Howard Kirschenbaum, co-author, Values Clarification

Rabbi Elkins has written another creative, useful, and user-friendly book that will help teachers, groups workers and Rabbis enrich their teaching of Jewish subject matter.

Audrey Friedman Marcus, Executive Vice-President, A.R.E. Publishing.

What a treat! Dov Elkins has compiled a rich collection of guided imagery scripts, with invaluable suggestions for implementation.

Dr. Mel Silberman, Prof. of Organizational Development, Temple Univ.

Dr. Elkins has compiled an exceptionally interesting and uplifting collection of essays and articles on the meaning and practice of the Jewish Sabbath. Readers of this book will be rewarded not just with new information, but with the kind of education that will help mold their character and forge their spiritual values.

Prof. Harold T. Shapiro, President, Princeton University

– Peter Bergson –
The Jewish Lobbyist Who Advocated To Save Jews During the Holocaust

Hillel Kook to the Rescue

When a group of Jews are in danger, fellow Jews around the world rally quickly to help rescue their endangered sisters and brothers.

The most famous Jewish scholar of the Middle Ages, Rabbi Moshe ben Maimon (known as Maimonides (1138-1204) wrote this in his Code of Jewish Law (Mishneh Torah):

> If one person is able to save another and does not save him, he transgresses the commandment *neither shalt thou stand idly by the blood of thy neighbor.*
>
> *(Leviticus 19:16)*

During the years of World War II (1939-1945), a very evil man, Adolf Hitler of Germany, decided to massacre every Jew in the world.

If more Jews in America had followed the advice of Maimonides, like Hillel Kook, many Jews might have been saved.

Unfortunately, for reasons that we can only try to understand, very little was done by American Jewry to help save the millions of Jews in Europe whose lives were in very grave danger.

Alas, by 1945, six million of our sisters and brothers were murdered by Hitler and his government.

How did this happen, and why didn't American Jews do more to prevent this horrible, unspeakable tragedy?

There are many views on this subject.

There was one Jew who, along with his friends and co-workers, exerted great efforts to try to save as many Jews as possible. His efforts were not as successful as he had wanted, but his work and his name deserve to be known by more people.

The man I am referring to was born Hillel Kook. When he left Palestine (today Israel) in the 1940s, he took the name by which he became known going forward – Peter Bergson. Because many people did not approve of his methods, he changed his name so that he would not embarrass his famous Uncle, Rabbi Abraham Isaac Kook.

Rabbi Abraham Isaac Kook was the first Ashkenazi Chief Rabbi of British Mandatory Palestine in the Land of Israel. He is considered to be one of the fathers of religious Zionism, and is known for founding the Mercaz HaRav Yeshiva.

Hillel Kook

Hillel Kook was born in the town of Kruk, Lithuania, in July 1915, during the First World War. He was born into a very famous and distinguished family. Hillel's father, Rabbi Dov Kook, was a well-known scholar and regional chief rabbi. The brother of Rabbi Dov Kook was even more famous than he was. Rabbi Abraham Isaac Kook eventually became the first chief rabbi of Palestine. Rabbi Abraham Isaac Kook is known to this day as one of the leading Jewish teachers, writers and spiritual leaders of the twentieth century.

Hillel's mother, Rebecca, was also descended from a very famous and highly respected family, the Schockens, who were wealthy merchants and members of the Hasidic Lubavitch group.

During the spring of 1915, when Rebecca was about to give birth to Hillel, the last of her eight children, the Russian military attacked the Jewish community. It was fairly common for Jews in Eastern Europe to suffer from pogroms (senseless attacks on Jewish communities). When Rabbi Dov Kook heard about the order to expel and harm the Jewish community, he took his large family and left. He and his wife were very fortunate, since Rebecca's family was wealthy enough to buy horses and carriages to leave their home before the pogrom began. They traveled long distances and ended up in southeast Ukraine, where there was a strong Jewish community.

In many surrounding towns, thousands of Jews were slaughtered. The Jews had no nation, no army, to protect them.

In one terrible event, the home of Rabbi Dov Kook was ransacked, so Rebecca fled, together with her little four-year-old son Hillel, and her four daughters, Batya, Sonya, Tzila and Nehamah. Another son, fifteen-year-old Nahum stayed in the house, and was shot by the attackers. When Rebecca found him, he was almost dead.

Rebecca warned Nahum:

Nahum, please try not to cry out, so none of the bad men will hear you.

Rebecca and her children hid in a cellar for hours, while the streets of the town were flowing with the blood of killed Jews.

"Mother," cried Hillel, "why are these bad men doing these horrible things to our fellow Jews? Is no one coming to stop them, and defend us?"

"Hillel," replied Rebecca, "I wish we had our own army, or a state of our own, with an army to protect us. Perhaps if we pray a lot, help will come."

Hillel was not satisfied. He dreamed of the day when Jews would have their own country, their own army, and be able to defend themselves. The dream had such a strong effect on Hillel's soul, that for the rest of his life, he worked to do whatever was possible to protect his people.

The Kook Family Moves to Palestine

Many rabbis and their students believed that the Messiah would come and bring all the Jews to Eretz Yisrael (the Land of Israel), and there would no longer be pogroms or any troubles for the Jews who lived there. Others, like Rabbi Abraham Isaac Kook, had a different idea. They believed that the Jewish people had to settle the Land of Israel, and after hard work, the Messiah would come and bring redemption.

Rabbi Abraham Isaac Kook left for Eretz Yisrael in 1904, and in 1921 he became Chief Rabbi of Palestine.

"Please follow me," the elder rabbi pleaded with his family. "It is not easy to live here, but if many of our family, and other families, will come and settle the land, we will build a wonderful and secure country."

Hillel's eldest brother, Rabbi Rafael Kook, was the first in his family to go up ("to make Aliyah") to live in Eretz Yisrael. Finally in 1925, he was able to arrange visas and housing for the other members of his family. Even though they had no comforts, such as flowing water or electricity, and they suffered from diseases like malaria and typhus, they were happy to finally be living in their ancestral homeland.

"Family," said her husband to Rebecca and their children, "life will be difficult for us for a long while, but hopefully in this homeland," continued Rabbi Dov Kook, "we will avoid the terrible pogroms that the nasty Russian government afflicted on us."

At age ten, young Hillel Kook started to study Torah in a Talmud Torah school. When he grew older, he studied in a school started by his uncle, Rabbi Abraham Isaac Kook. Such schools for the older students were called "yeshivahs" or in Hebrew, "yeshivot."

The yeshivah where Hillel studied was different from other yeshivot. The language which the teachers used in this yeshivah was Hebrew, not Yiddish. Other rabbis thought that Hebrew should be reserved for prayer, and that when speaking, Yiddish should be the language. This yeshivah was more modern and open-minded.

The first friend whom Hillel met in the yeshivah was a captivating youth, a few years older than him. Hillel was thin and frail. His new friend, David Raziel, taught Hillel many important skills, including boxing, and subjects like philosophy.

"I want you to learn about Zionism," said David to Hillel. Zionism was the new movement of Jewish nationalism, promoted by Theodor Herzl. Zionism encouraged Jews to return to their homeland, Eretz Yisrael. It spread to Jewish

Theodor Herzl.

communities in Europe and America, and all around the world.

David Raziel, one of the founders and commander of the "Etzel" underground organization, was killed in action during World War II, while serving with the British military.

Time passed and David and Hillel left the yeshivah and enrolled in schools that taught secular subjects, such as science, mathematics, literature, art and music.

Hillel now saw himself as a Zionist, who wanted to fight for the rights of his people to be free, strong and independent.

Despite the fact that Hillel now lived in his ancestral homeland, there were still problems of safety. Palestinian Arabs were not happy to see Jews returning to their own home. Jewish leaders tried to persuade the local Arabs that they wanted to live in peace, as friendly neighbors. They helped the Arabs economically by hiring them, teaching them modern agricultural techniques, providing medical care, etc. But the Arabs

The Mufti: Mohammed Amin al-Husseini.

refused to listen. One Arab leader, called the "Mufti," named Haj Amin al-Husseini, who was the political and Muslim religious leader of the Palestinian Arabs, encouraged his followers to attack Jews.

In 1929, al-Husseini organized a riot against Jews praying at the Kotel (the western wall of the compound of

Hebron synagogue desecrated during the 1929 Arab riots.

the ancient Temple of biblical days). Over 500 Jews were murdered there, in Hebron, Safed, and several other places during this period. Hillel remembered the pogroms he witnessed as a young lad.

Hillel's friend, David Raziel, encouraged him to join a new group called the Haganah (the Zionist military organization). Members of the Haganah were taught to fight and use weapons to defend themselves.

At the end of World War I, the British conquered

Foreign Office,

November 2nd, 1917.

Dear Lord Rothschild,

I have much pleasure in conveying to you, on behalf of His Majesty's Government, the following declaration of sympathy with Jewish Zionist aspirations which has been submitted to, and approved by, the Cabinet

'His Majesty's Government view with favour the establishment in Palestine of a national home for the Jewish people, and will use their best endeavours to facilitate the achievement of this object, it being clearly understood that nothing shall be done which may prejudice the civil and religious rights of existing non-Jewish communities in Palestine, or the rights and political status enjoyed by Jews in any other country"

I should be grateful if you would bring this declaration to the knowledge of the Zionist Federation.

The Balfour Declaration, November 2, 1917.

Palestine and took control over the land in place of the Turks, who had previously ruled for several centuries. Some British leaders understood the need for Jews to return to their biblical homeland. The British government issued the famous "Balfour Declaration," which stated:

"His Majesty's Government view with favour the establishment in Palestine of a national home for the Jewish people."

However, they were persuaded by Arab leaders to prevent Jews from owning weapons.

Ze'ev Jabotinsky.

Jews did not accept this ruling, and secretly began acquiring arms and were trained to use them to protect themselves.

By the time he was eighteen, Hillel devoted his life to the activities of the *Irgun Z'vai Leumi* (the National Military Organization), an underground army formed as a Haganah splinter group. The Haganah was the core army that evolved into today's modern Israel Defense Force (IDF). Hillel and his friends were strongly influenced by the writings of the Russian Zionist leader, Vladimir Ze'ev Jabotinsky, who was a strong advocate of the establishment of a Jewish state.

The logo of the Irgun. The organization was also referred to as Etzel, an acronym of the Hebrew initials, or by the abbreviation IZL.

By 1936, the membership of the Irgun had grown from a few hundred to two thousand. Hillel, David and other friends, became increasingly devoted to matters relating to self-defense. They became a tightly-knit group of like-minded friends, with a passionate cause: preventing the killing of their people, and working toward the founding of a Jewish nation.

Hillel and his comrades were highly disciplined. They did physical training, and devoted most of their time to the cause of Jewish self-defense and Jewish nationalism. This strong discipline was very helpful in preparing them for their most important tasks – which we shall discuss soon.

Meanwhile, they found ways to get around the British rules of keeping Jews from immigrating to Eretz Yisrael, and smuggling arms into the country.

Between the years 1937 and 1940 – in just three years, the Irgun succeeded in secretly smuggling tens of thousands of European Jews into Palestine.

Unfortunately, this was a small percentage of the number of Jews who would soon lose their lives during the worst tragedy in Jewish history.

The White Paper

The major goal for the many millions of Jews trapped in Europe, prior to Hitler's implementation of his plan to murder all the world's Jews, was to escape to Eretz Yisrael (known before 1948 as Palestine).

As noted above, following World War I control over Palestine was given by the League of Nations to Great Britain. Britain was given total control over the numbers and the type of people who could enter Palestine.

British Jews protest against immigration restrictions to Palestine after Kristallnacht in 1938.

This "British Mandate" over Palestine was the sole authority over the gates of entry into the land.

Unfortunately, the leaders of the British Mandate were strongly influenced by Palestinian Arabs. The latter were successful in persuading British officials to prevent large numbers into the land.

On May 17, 1939, the British government issued an official document called "The White Paper," which limited Jewish immigration to Palestine to 75,000, over a period of five years.

In addition, the White Paper ruled that Jews were not allowed to buy more than five percent of the land.

Jewish leaders were furious at this ruling.

It meant that once Hitler began the extermination of European Jewry, the gates out of Europe and into the Promised Land were closed.

David Raziel and Hillel Kook came up with a plan to try to overcome this horrible, evil decree.

David told Hillel, his close friend and co-worker:

We must do something radical, something powerful, to persuade the British government to annul this evil decree.

These two brave and daring leaders decided to take unprecedented action to force the British leaders to relent.

In response, Hillel said to David:

I agree. We must do something drastic. We cannot sit idly by and let the vile British leaders carry out a decree that will condemn to death hundreds, perhaps thousands, or even, Heaven forbid, millions of our people.

Rabbis and public figures demonstrate against the White Paper in Tel Aviv in May 1939. The marchers included the chief rabbis of Tel Aviv, Rabbi Ben Zion Meir Hai Uziel and Rabbi Moshe Avigdor Amiel and the mayor of Tel Aviv.

The plan that David Raziel and Hillel Kook, together with other wise colleagues in the Irgun High Command in Jerusalem came up with is one that they never dreamed they would suggest.

But dangerous times demand unusual actions.

They decided to attack British targets, causing severe damage to property and even individuals.

Attacking British buildings, offices, and even British officers, was not a decision taken lightly. But when the fate of a huge number of Jewish lives was at stake, they felt they had few choices.

Two More Triggers

Two other tragic events encouraged David Raziel and Hillel Kook to proceed with their plan to attack British targets.

On May 13, 1939, the ship SS St. Louis set sail from Hamburg, Germany, to Cuba, carrying 937 passengers, most of whom were Jewish refugees seeking asylum from Nazi persecution in Germany. The ship dropped anchor at 4 a.m. on May 27 at the Havana, Cuba, harbor. The Cuban government refused to accept the foreign refugees, even though they held legal tourist visas to Cuba. The ship's captain then ordered the ship to attempt docking in nearby Florida. When the matter was raised in Washington D.C., the American Secretary of State, Cordell Hull, advised

Passengers on the SS St. Louis.

The SS St. Louis returned to Europe in June 1939, after the ship was denied docking permission in Cuba and the United States for the passengers, primarily Jewish, to disembark.

American president Franklin Roosevelt, not to accept the Jewish refugees. The president readily agreed.

American journalists called the St. Louis affair one of the most disgraceful events in the history of America, a country which took pride in accepting refugees and oppressed victims.

This was a moment when the many American Jewish organizations whose mission was to save endangered Jews might have fought diligently to find a safe haven for these victims of Nazi oppression. Their timid reaction to this case was emblematic of worse things to come. Afraid of arousing more antisemitism in America, they decided to remain passive and silent. Neither did they wish to offend President Roosevelt, whom most Americans admired greatly. That was more important to them than saving Jewish lives.

Historians think the fate of the SS St. Louis was a test case for the Nazis. Seeing that the democratic countries of the world were not concerned about the fate of the Jewish people, Nazi Germany concluded that they could proceed with their diabolic plan to exterminate all Jews – a plan they named "The Final Solution."

While a small number of the passengers found refuge in various European countries, only the ones who were accepted in England were saved; most eventually perished in Hitler's death camps.

A second failed plan was a proposal by a few members of the United States Congress, called the "Wagner-Rogers Bill," named for the Senator and Congressman who proposed the bill. The bill proposed admitting 20,000 German refugee children to the United States, outside of immigration quotas. The bill referred to "German" children instead of "Jewish" children, since the idea of bringing Jews to America was a very unpopular one. Antisemitism in America was strong at that time.

The bill was enthusiastically supported by many leading Americans, such as former president Herbert Hoover, and the famous singer Eddie Cantor.

Here is another instance when one would have hoped that American Jewish leaders and organizations would have strongly supported such a bill. But again the timidity of American Jews prevailed. They were afraid that speaking out in favor of saving Jewish lives would make it seem that they were more loyal to their people, their Jewish roots, than to their nation, America. This idea, called "dual loyalty," loyalty to the Jewish people as well as to America, often caused most of American Jewry to be afraid to act.

The result was that the Wagner-Rogers bill never came to a vote in the U.S. Congress. It died from fear.

In the next chapter Hillel Kook becomes a "Clark Kent"

and his "Superman" outfit takes over. From now on he is no longer "Hillel Kook," but is transformed almost magically, into "Peter Bergson."

Hillel Kook Becomes Peter Bergson

Because of his work with the "illegal" organization to bring more Jews to Eretz Yisrael, hoping to save them from the Nazi murderers, the British cast Hillel as a dangerous person. His activities marked him as a rebel and an enemy of British policy.

Knowing that his safety was endangered, Hillel decided to take a new name – Peter Bergson.

There was another reason for changing his name. The Kooks were a distinguished family. His father, Rabbi Dov Kook, was well known as a great scholar and teacher. His father's brother, Rabbi Abraham Isaac Kook, revered in Orthodox circles, had been Chief Rabbi of the British Mandate Palestine. In order not to embarrass the Kook family, Hillel thought it wise to avoid any connection with the Kook name.

Hillel Kook / Peter Bergson.

Thinking about selecting a new name, Hillel took the name "Bergson," since his father's first name was "Dov," which means "bear" in Hebrew. So

"Bergson" was "the son of a bear."

From then forward, Hillel Kook became Peter Bergson. Now the British would cast a suspicious eye whenever the name of Peter Bergson was seen.

In his new role, Peter Bergson followed the wishes of his mentor, Ze'ev Jabotinsky. Jabotinsky's idea was to create an army of Jewish soldiers, and to create a Jewish state. To aid in this effort, Peter raised funds in Europe and later in the United States.

Peter arrived in America in 1940, at age twenty-five, but his mustache gave him the appearance of someone older and experienced. What he found in America was a Jewish community absorbed in becoming assimilated into the surrounding culture, and with too little concern about the problems of Judaism, and their brothers and sisters facing enormous dangers throughout Europe.

There was not enough interest in the movement to create a Jewish state in Palestine – Zionism. Peter had his work cut out for him.

Besides the apathy of the American Jewish community, American Jews faced virulent antisemitism. One popular national American magazine, *Fortune*, in its issue of April 1939, published a poll stating that the majority of Americans were opposed to admitting Jewish refugees into America. They also commented that Hitler and his German-American followers can safely assume that "Americans don't like Jews much better than do the Nazis."

In July 1942, a Gallup poll showed that one of every six Americans thought that Hitler was "doing the right thing" to the Jews.

Peter's New Enemy

As mentioned, when one would expect American Jewish organizations to arise to the saving of Jewish lives, their fear and timidity prevented any action on their part. For Peter, one of the most difficult individuals he had to struggle with was Rabbi Stephen Wise, head of the American Jewish Congress, and founder of a well-known school to train Reform rabbis, The Jewish Institute of Religion.

Rabbi Wise was a tall, handsome, eloquent speaker, with a stentorian voice. One of his main efforts for the Jewish people was to establish a Jewish state in Palestine after the war was concluded. Unfortunately, his single-minded efforts to help create a Jewish state blinded him to the serious problem of saving millions of Jewish lives whom the Nazis were planning to exterminate.

Rabbi Wise's popularity, being spokesperson for several

Stephen Samuel Wise.

important Jewish groups, and being a powerful orator, continued to grow. As he became more and more popular, his blindness to the welfare of European Jewry caused great harm to the cause of the survival of millions of his fellow Jews.

Rabbi Wise's need for importance and political power created friction between him and other rabbis and Jewish political leaders. He was even jealous of the efforts of Peter Bergson and his group of associates, since their ideas seemed to have been more successful than his own.

One significant example demonstrates the failure of Rabbi Wise. In the mind of Rabbi Wise, he had a close relationship with President Franklin Roosevelt, and that seemed to him more important than anything else. When it came time to speak up, and organize in a way that the American government and population would pay attention and take positive action to save Jewish lives, Rabbi Wise often took the path of least resistance. His approach was "hush hush," we don't want to offend the president, or stir up antisemitism (which, as mentioned above, was growing strongly in America in the 1940s).

In August 1940, a large and important group of traditional rabbis decided to persuade many large Jewish organizations to save 2,800 rabbis and yeshivah students in Lithuania by insisting that the U.S. State Department grant non-quota visas for them.

At that time there was a conference of several major Jewish organizations. Rabbi Wise was the main speaker. Acting with great caution, as usual, Rabbi Wise said that the United States could only absorb around 500 religious leaders. He thought it imprudent to pressure the government. At such a crucial crossroad in Jewish history, this timid plan was a very bad idea, he said. Once again Rabbi Wise put his relationship with President Roosevelt before the needs of his people.

Peter Bergson, like Rabbi Wise, had a great deal of charisma. He was extremely bright, good looking, and had a knack for attracting able people to assist him

Peter's approach was the opposite of that of Rabbi Wise. He deemed it necessary to create a great deal of publicity and propaganda. He was able to persuade scores of U.S. Senators, congresspersons, some members of the War Department, members of the President's cabinet, and a number of well-known intellectuals, to his way of thinking.

In May 1941, Peter lost his best friend, David Raziel, who was killed when the Germans bombed oil fields in Habbaniyah, Iraq. At the time, Raziel was working with the British army. It took Peter a long time to get over this great loss. After a period of grieving, he began to work at the creation of a Jewish army to help the allies fight the Germans. With friends and co-workers, in December 1941, he established the Committee for a Jewish Army.

To launch this new military group, Peter organized a convention in Washington, D.C. Peter was named National Director, and his committee members included thirteen senators (Including Senator Harry Truman, a future president), several retired generals and admirals, leading clergymen, writers and entertainers.

During the next six months Peter and his co-workers raised funds to purchase scores of full-page magazine and newspaper advertisements, asking people to join the new Jewish army. One ad in particular, in *The New York Times*, in January 1942, entitled "Jews Fight for the Right to Fight," attracted great attention. In today's world we see political ads in newspapers fairly often, but in Peter's day this was a novelty. It was an excellent example of Peter's creative approach to get his message across.

Many newspaper columnists praised the Jewish army advertisement. One newspaper, unfortunately, held an opposing view. *The New York Times* publisher, Arthur Sulzberger, wanted no part of Zionism. *The New York Times* gave almost no attention to news about Jews. The very word "Jew" appearing in his paper was annoying to Sulzberger. Similarly, other assimilationist Jews felt the same way.

Ironically, Senator Edwin Johnson of Colorado, and other Congressional colleagues, including non-Jews, became strong supporters of Peter and his friends, who became known as the "Bergson Boys."

A full-page advertisement in *The Washington Post* of May 25, 1942, was signed by many distinguished non-Jews and Jews, including the famous theologians Reinhold Niebuhr and Paul Tillich, the civil rights activist A. Philip Randolph, and many other well-known individuals of various backgrounds.

Despite valiant efforts on the part of the Bergson group, American and British leaders did not favor any part of a plan to save Jewish lives to include assistance from the Jews living in Palestine.

Still, the Bergson group persisted in finding new and strong methods to make whatever efforts they could in trying to save as many Jews as they could.

Only at the end of the war did the British make a token gesture and allowed the establishment of a Jewish military unit, which was far too little and much too late. In all their communications they avoided the word "Jew" when it came

Hitler and his Nazis.

to referring to Jewish refugees, and called them "Poles" or "refugees."

The British relented as the tragedy of the murder of millions of Jews in Europe by Hitler and his Nazis became well known, agreeing to the establishment of the Jewish Brigade.

Apart from its contribution to the war effort against Nazi Germany, the brigade fulfilled two historic functions. One, it gave great strength to the staying power of the Jewish survivors and refugees in Europe when they saw a "Jewish" unit fighting against the Nazis. Two, the experience these soldiers gained in military organization and in battle was invaluable, as many of the brigade soldiers would go on to become the foundation of the new Israel Defense Force.

Enter Ben Hecht and Friends

Despite the opposition the Bergson Boys faced, some amazing high-profile individuals would soon come to their aid. Enter Ben Hecht.

The friendship of Peter Bergson and reporter Ben Hecht in Spring 1941 changed the entire program of the Bergson Boys. How did this happen?

Ben Hecht was America's leading screenwriter in the

Ben Hecht.

1930s. His reputation as a writer and reporter made him one of the leading spokespersons in America.

How did he and Peter become close friends and colleagues, even though Hecht was twenty years Peter's senior?

Hecht was not an observant Jew, but he cared deeply about the welfare of the Jewish people. When he heard of the horrors of Hitler's massacre of European Jewry, he became shocked that little or nothing was being done by the major American Jewish organizations. So he did what all good writers would do when a major national scandal appears.

He wrote a powerful, critical column in a leading journal lambasting those organizations for not speaking out about this incredible crime against Jewry and humanity.

When Peter read this tough newspaper column he turned to his friends:

I must meet this Ben Hecht. He sounds like just the right person who could help us in our cause.

And so Peter set about to try and arrange such a meeting. He wrote Hecht a letter asking for an opportunity to explore their mutual interest – saving Jewish lives.

Peter was happily surprised when he received a positive reply from the famous writer, inviting him to a meeting at the posh 21 Club of Manhattan. Hecht quickly discovered that he was meeting the political head of the soon-to-be notorious Palestinian underground called the *Irgun Z'vai Leumi* (The National Military Organization).

After their initial meeting, both men were mutually impressed. Peter quickly recognized that Hecht was very bright, well-educated and sophisticated. Though he was a proud Jew, he knew very little about Zionism and the plans to create a Jewish state in the ancient homeland. Peter was thrilled to finally meet an American Jew who exhibited his great pride in his Jewishness. Most of the American Jews whom Peter had met until now were assimilated and not educated either in Judaism or Zionism. Nor did they care very much about increasing their awareness of these areas of their lives.

Just as Peter was impressed with Ben Hecht, so Hecht was impressed with Peter, though Peter was only twenty-six-years old. Hecht looked upon this young Palestinian Jew as a "Hebrew hero."

Ben Hecht was a great asset to the Jewish people from the time he met Peter Bergson. Of course, he was already famous for having written thirty-five books, and seventy classic screenplays. This talented, creative and famous American cultural hero was now signed up to follow the ideas of the Bergson Boys. Hecht saw Peter and his crew as "Jews of gallantry."

His view aligned with Peter's, that leading American Jews were flagrantly silent.

Among other important successes achieved by Hecht was that he persuaded David O. Selznick, a famous film producer, screenwriter and film studio executive – best known for producing "Gone With the Wind" – to sign a telegram sent to a thousand Hollywood personalities. Most of those who received the telegram did not agree that there should be a Jewish army, but a few important people did agree. One of those who supported the Bergson Boys and their plans was the famous comic actor, Charlie Chaplin, one of he most important figures in the film industry. Other nationally important individuals joined the cause later. We will discuss them in coming chapters.

Ben Hecht's efforts to support the Bergson Boys and their idea of an army of Jewish fighters to aid the allies in fighting Germany, found some opposition from Rabbi Wise and the American Jewish Congress.

Since the Bergson advertisements attacked the U.S. State Department policy, those who opposed the Bergson group claimed that anyone who attacked the U.S. government would arouse the antisemites.

Another very important supporter of the Bergson program was a world-renowned artist, Arthur Szyk. Szyk's drawings illustrated the Bergson group's publications and advertisements. Szyk later illustrated Israel's Declaration of Independence, when the State of Israel was born. Many of his previous illustrations, such as his famous Passover Haggadah, became world famous. His reputation grew so strongly that many critics considered him one of the greatest artists who ever lived.

Like Bergson, Szyk was deeply shocked by the timid attitude of the major Jewish establishment. "The old leaders," he wrote in great sorrow and anger, "have changed from lovers of Zion into chasers after prestige and are ready to stake all ... provided they remain unchallenged in their position of dubious eminence. Condemn them [the young Bergson group] if you must, but pray to the Almighty for their success."

Yet another person drawn to Peter Bergson and his group was the famous composer, Kurt Weill, who achieved great acclaim for his collaboration on *The Threepenny Opera*. Weill wrote most of the music for the shows that the Bergson Boys staged around the country to publicize his message.

Many other well-known Christians and Jews joined in when they realized how important the cause of saving Jewish lives was; some out of pure humanitarian instincts and social responsibility, others because of their loyalty to the Jewish people.

Some of such well-known personalities included Clare Booth Luce, Dorothy Parker, former president Herbert Hoover, actor Jimmy Durante, impresario and composer Billy Rose, and many others.

In the U.S. Congress there were many supporters, but two stand out for their deep devotion and strong commitment to this sacred work: Senator Guy Gillette of Iowa and Congressman Will Rogers, Jr. of California. Senator Gillette gave a speech expressing his commitment to the cause,

(R-L) Bergson, Congressman Will Rogers, Jr. and Senator Guy Gillette, 1944.

saying that it was not "just a Jewish or Hebrew problem, but an urgent question for all humanity."

Congressman Will Rogers Jr., the son of the famous humorist, had a long history in involvement in struggles for human rights, and was strongly influenced by Peter Bergson. He worked very hard to persuade President Roosevelt to establish a special agency to save Jews.

Rogers wrote that Peter Bergson and Ben Hecht convinced me "that a mass murder was going on ... and I thought that every activity and every action and every wheel should be turned to try to get these people out." Rogers considered his work with the Bergson Boys one of the highlights of his life. "They were an alert, wonderful group, with a great moral fervor."

Bergson's Efforts Take A Dark Turn

The valiant efforts of Peter Bergson (alias Hillel Kook) were never as successful as they might have, and should have been. His dream of saving Jewish lives often faced serious obstacles.

Rabbi Stephen Wise even went so far as to ask his friend, J. Edgar Hoover, head of the FBI, to look into the efforts of the Bergsons. Observing that Bergson was receiving great attention in his efforts and had wider and wider appeal among important American leaders, Rabbi Wise became very jealous and constantly increased his efforts to try to downplay his work.

Meanwhile, Adolf Hitler, with his insane plans to destroy the Jewish people, appointed one of his military henchmen, Reinhard Heydrich, of the notorious SS (Schutzstaffel, a major paramilitary organization under Adolf Hitler and the Nazi Party in Nazi Germany, and later throughout German-occupied Europe, which became the elite guard of the Nazi Reich), to convene a meeting of fourteen heads of agencies to plan for the "Final Solution."

The Final Solution was the code-word for the mass extermination of the Jews. Already hundreds of thousands of Jews had been shot by the SS units, but now the massacre was to be systematic and complete.

News of the Final Solution was slow in reaching those outside Europe.

One individual, Gerhart Riegner, who was the Geneva, Switzerland representative of the World Jewish Congress, received information in August 1942, from a reliable source, regarding the Final Solution. Riegner attempted to pass on this horrendous information to a British parliament leader, and asked that it be passed on to Rabbi Wise. Finally, by the end of the month, Rabbi Wise received the information.

When the news reached the U.S. State Department, they persuaded Rabbi Wise to withhold the news "until they could confirm it."

Years later Elie Wiesel, perhaps the world's leading survivor of the *Shoah* (Holocaust) shared his shock and dismay about Wise's timidity.

Wiesel wrote:

How could ... Jewish leaders pledge silence? How is it that they did not cry out in despair? More important, more disturbing is this question: What happened after Rabbi Wise was released from his pledge? Not much. Not much at all. Did he and the other Jewish leaders proclaim hunger strikes to the end? Did they organize daily marches to the White House? They should have shaken heaven and earth, echoing the agony of their doomed brethren taken in by Roosevelt's personality they in a way became accomplices to his inaction.

The U.S. State Department finally confirmed the frightening reports in November 1942, and permitted Rabbi Wise to release the news. Rabbi Wise called a press conference in Washington, but the media made little of the

---

The Riegner Telegram
by Christopher R. Browning

The Riegner telegram relayed information of a plan under consideration at Hitler's headquarters to kill all the Jews of Europe in one blow in the autumn of 1942... Hitler and Himmler did in fact make a vital decision in mid-July 1942 to intensify the mass murder of European Jewry, and Eduard Sahulte relayed to Riegner precisely what Himmler would have been speaking about immediately thereafter during his visit to Auschwitz-Birkenau on July 17-18.

http://hgs.oxfordjournals.org/cgi/content/abstract/10/1/3

---

news, such that *The New York Times* and *The Washington Post,* both owned by Jews, did not even take the trouble to send their reporters.

The result was that the news that two million Jews had already been slaughtered ended up as a minor story on page ten of *The New York Times. The Washington Post* also buried the story in its back pages.

While the main sources of news in the American press did not consider the genocide of the Jewish people, now about to commence, as greatly significant, this shocking news was not permitted to pass so easily in the mind of Peter Bergson.

In prior reports, news of the destroying of Jewish bodies was thought of by many as perhaps either not important, or just a rumor similar to rumors that were spread during World War I. Peter Bergson, on the other hand, did not take this news lightly. To him, it was shocking beyond belief.

The seemingly hushed message struck Peter like a thunderbolt. For this activist, a highly intelligent twenty-seven-year-old Palestinian Jew, the news was life-changing.

Peter made an urgent telephone call to Assistant

Peter Bergson did not take the news lightly of the genocide of the Jewish people. To him, this was shocking beyond belief and he did everything he could to mobilize the American leadership to help save European Jewry.

Secretary of State Adolph Berle and insisted on meeting with him immediately. Peter asked Berle if this important, almost unbelievable news of the extermination of the Jews of Europe was true.

"Yes," replied Berle. "There can no longer be any doubt that Hitler's 'Final Solution' is now being implemented. Two million Jews have already been massacred, and the Nazis are now planning to murder the rest of European Jewry."

"What are you going to do about it?" asked Peter.

"What can we do?" replied Berle, shrugging his shoulders, to show little concern. "My colleagues here in the U.S. State Department believe, as I do, that there is nothing we can do for the Jews in Europe until after we win the war."

"If it were Americans, or maybe gentiles in Europe,"

replied Peter, "you would not be shrugging your shoulders in such a carefree way. Since it's a matter of Jewish lives," continued Peter, increasing in anger and frustration, "you don't really think of this as your problem."

"Mr. Bergson," said Berle, "if I thought I could stop the Nazis tomorrow, maybe I could help the Jews. But I doubt very much if that is in my power, or anybody's power."

"Well maybe you don't think that anything can be done," shouted Peter in even greater anger and frustration, "but I have a talented and important group of active American and Palestinian Jews who believe otherwise, and we are going to do whatever we can, with, or without the help of the American government."

Peter was not one to sit on his hands and do nothing when the lives of millions of his Jewish sisters and brothers were in danger.

He traveled from Washington to New York that evening, and for many days met with his associates and made plans to encourage the U.S. government to take this matter more seriously, and act as if there were a terrible emergency – which indeed there was.

One of the major decisions made at this time brought the efforts of the Bergson group to an entirely new mode of thinking and acting. Until now, most of their efforts were directed toward creating a Jewish army to help the allies fight and defeat the Nazis. From that point on, they reversed course and moved in a totally different direction. They set aside their efforts to create an army and look forward to building a Jewish state in Eretz Yisrael, and decided to put all their labors into saving Jewish lives.

In the Fall of 1942, the Bergson group began to assemble almost two thousand signatures of prominent individuals for a "Proclamation on the Moral Rights of the Stateless and Palestinian Jews." Mostly composed by Pierre van Paassen, a famous journalist and Unitarian minister, one of several important Christian advocates for Zionism, the proclamation read:

We shall no longer witness with pity alone, and with passive sympathy, the calculated extermination of the ancient Jewish People by the barbarous Nazis.

The proclamation was signed by twenty-seven senators, twenty governors, and hundreds of other political leaders, leading military men, clergymen, labor leaders, actors and artists, and included an illustration by Arthur Szyk, displaying a Jewish soldier with a tommy gun assisting a few elderly people. The very large advertisement appeared in the *New York Times* and many other newspapers around the country.

In reaction to these ads, the U.S. government urged the Jewish community to quiet the matter. On December 1, 1942, Rabbi Wise bragged in a letter to President Roosevelt:

"I succeeded together with the heads of other Jewish organizations in keeping [the Riegner report] out of the press."

The Bergson Boys did not sit idly during these dark days. Seeing what the Jewish leaders were not doing, they decided to spring into action.

The Bergson Boys Go Into Action

When the Bergsonites realized that the leading Jewish leaders and the American government were doing far too little to save Jewish lives, they began to make dramatic efforts to grab the attention of the American public.

They began a large number of important efforts, such as lobbying government officials, mass rallies, pageants and concerts. This, of course, aroused the anger of the major Jewish organizations, who called the Bergson people "circus show people." Realizing that the Bergsonite efforts were successful, they began to copy some of them. They thought of planning a rally in Madison Square Garden, but Rabbi Wise at first vetoed the idea, though later he did hold his own rally. When Rabbi Wise heard of the pageant, he called Ben Hecht and said:

I have read your pageant script, and I disapprove of it. I must ask you to cancel this pageant and discontinue all your further activities on behalf of the Jews. If you wish hereafter to work for the Jewish cause, you will please consult me and let me advise you.

Hearing this, Hecht hung up the phone and abruptly ended the conversation.

Hecht went ahead and planned his massive pageant, "We Will Never Die." On March 9, over 40,000 people filled Madison Square Garden to witness the performance presented by Ben Hecht and his talented theater friends and many well-known artists.

The scene was captivating and dramatic. A narrator standing next to two huge Tablets of the Ten Commandments, proclaimed:

"Before our eyes has appeared the strange and awesome picture of a folk being put to death, of a great and ancient people in whose veins have lingered for so long the earliest words and image of God.... They shall never die, though they were slaughtered with no weapon in their hands. Though they fill the dark land of Europe with the smoke of their massacre, they shall never die."

Scene from "We Will Never Die".

New York Governor Thomas Dewey was persuaded by Billy Rose to proclaim the day of the pageant an official day of mourning.

When he found out about this proclamation, Rabbi Wise led a group of a dozen well-known Jewish leaders to the state capitol in Albany to attempt to dissuade Governor Dewey from such a proclamation, warning the governor that he might lose New York City's Jewish vote if he sided with the Bergson group. Dewey wisely refused and made the proclamation.

Despite the efforts of Rabbi Wise to prevent the pageant from being presented in several cities, it was staged in New York, and following that on tour in six major cities. It was an instant success, attracting nationwide press coverage.

The pageant at Constitution Hall, near the White House in Washington D.C., the city's largest concert hall, hit just the right chord.

Eleanor Roosevelt, the wife of President Roosevelt, attended, along with diplomats from forty countries, hundreds of members of congress, and scores of other well-known personalities.

In Mrs. Roosevelt's nationally syndicated column, she wrote:

"No one who heard each group come forward and give the story of what happened to it at the hands of a ruthless military will ever forget the haunting words, 'Remember us!' "

The U.S. Senator from Colorado, Edward Johnson, who was chairman of the Bergson committee, spoke at the pageant in Constitution Hall.

Senator Johnson declared:

"The conspiracy of silence which surrounded the Jewish disaster in Europe is definitely broken... therefore it will be sinful if we do not agree upon a policy of action to save the millions who survive."

The Bergson committee did not stop after the success of the pageants. They proceeded to place advertisements in many newspapers, titled "Action – Not Pity, Can Save Millions Now!"

This advertisement ran in The New York Times on February 8, 1943.

On April 5, 1943, the Bergson group placed a full-page ad in *The Washington Post,* containing many specific steps for the rescue of Jews in Eastern Europe. Mainly their idea was to transfer Jews from countries under the control of the Nazis, such as Hungary and Rumania, to neutral countries – until they could find a more permanent residence.

Again, Rabbi Wise acted to prevent this plan from being successful. Some say that the head of the FBI, J. Edgar Hoover, sent a report to the Department of Justice, claiming that the Bergson group was led by "a group of thoroughly disreputable Communist Zionists." Among those he listed were Ben Hecht, composer Arnold Schoenberg, Max Lerner, and other distinguished Americans.

Emergency Conference

When it seemed more and more likely that the U.S. government was not concerned about the saving of Jewish lives, the Bergsonites conceived of another, more urgent plan. They decided to implement what became known as the "Emergency Conference to Save the Jewish People of Europe", for the summer of 1943.

Peter told his colleagues: "I think our main goal now should be to urge the U.S. government to create a special agency to achieve our objective of saving European Jews."

As soon as Rabbi Wise got wind of this new plan, he did whatever he could to prevent it, and let the State Department know of his views.

"This idea has no chance of success," Wise informed his friends at the State Department. Wise also contacted other friends to lend their weight to preventing this plan from succeeding.

Despite efforts to constrain him, Peter proceeded with his

plan, and enlisted a large number of important individuals to help him. These included several U.S. Senators and other highly-placed individuals. One of the most important people helping Peter was William Randolph Hearst, who had developed America's largest newspaper chain. Hearst's thirty-four newspapers totally supported the Emergency Conference and other ideas which Peter suggested.

Hearst emphasized Peter's central argument:

Remember, Americans, this is not a Jewish problem. It is a human problem.

The Emergency Conference met in New York on July 20, 1943. Chairing the Conference were two highly thought of national leaders, Senator Edward Johnson and prominent educator and journalist, Max Lerner. Some fifteen hundred people participated in the event.

During the six days during which the conference was held, nine important proposals were discussed for the rescue and refuge of Jews in danger.

Following the conference, Max Lerner published an article in a widely read journal, entitled, "What about the Jews, FDR?" In the article, Lerner condemned the British and American governments for their unhelpful and useless policies.

Lerner wrote:

Neither government recognizes that any Jewish problem exists. Both governments talk of the Jews as Polish nationals, or Czech nationals, or Hungarian nationals. Yet the fact remains that while Czechs are killed by the hundreds, Jews in Czechoslovakia are killed by the tens of thousands.

Lerner continued to emphasize that they were killed as Jews. Max Lerner was very positively impressed by Peter Bergson, even though Peter was a very young man. He told his friends:

Young Bergson had one of the best natural public relations talents that I have ever seen. And he had much more as well – a stunningly clear vision of what was happening in the Holocaust and a hard determination to act on it.

Following the Emergency Conference, those present decided to become a permanent group known as "The Emergency Committee to Save the Jewish People of Europe". Its goal was to present recommendations to Congress, government officials and the President, as well as to the general public.

One of the first things Peter did was to meet with State Department officials to press for the government to discuss some rescue ideas for European Jewry. The response was lukewarm. He then asked that Congress pass a resolution stating that there should be a special government agency to deal with the issue.

At the same time, the major Zionist organizations were mainly concerned about helping to promote the creation of a Jewish state. In late August 1943, there was a meeting of the Zionist organizations at the Waldorf-Astoria Hotel in New York City. Again, they discussed ways to promote a Jewish state, and barely mentioned the possibilities of rescue, until, under great pressure, they finally did create a rescue committee. They complained that the Bergson resolution omitted any reference to a Jewish state.

While the Zionist conference focused solely on proposals

for fostering the creation of a Jewish state in Palestine, one delegate, Robert P. Goldman of Cincinnati, challenged the other delegates with a fiery speech of condemnation.

Goldman said:

The immediate problem is rescue and I don't care what else you say or how you characterize it, or what you say about me for saying it, that is the immediate problem and that is the problem we should be concerned with.

Of course, Goldman's words fell on deaf ears. However, one other delegate agreed with Goldman, and said this:

The first task should be to save the Jews for whom Palestine is needed. By waiting till the last moment to discuss this question and bypassing stereotyped resolutions the leaders of the conference gave a signal to the powerful ministries that nothing can be done and that we have to wait till the war is over.

The Bergson group focused their energies from summer, 1943, until the duration of the war, on possibilities of rescue. They placed full-page ads in major newspapers throughout America.

An advertisement in *The New York Times* in August 1943, stated:

We all stand before the bar of humanity; history and God. We will all be judged if we do not create the machinery to save the Jewish people of Europe.

The Bergson group fought this battle for the rest of the

war. Fortunately, unlike the major Zionist organizations, they had help from some very important people.

One extremely important supporter of the Bergson group was Congressman Will Rogers, Jr.

Rogers wrote to his colleagues:

The big trouble – a fatal trouble – is that no one agency, no single man, has been given the entire responsibility for this job of saving the Jews. The lack of a clear goal has resulted in confusion and buck-passing, which spells utter inaction, which is the reason that a special agency is urgently needed.

Peter had several meetings with Eleanor Roosevelt, the wife of the President, in August 1943. Mrs. Roosevelt agreed to do act on two points.

- Point One: Broadcast a shortwave radio message to the Jews of Europe on behalf of the Emergency Committee.
- Point Two: Transmit to her husband, President Roosevelt, a recommendation of the Emergency Conference emphasizing the need for a rescue agency.

President Roosevelt told Mrs. Roosevelt's secretary, "I do not think this needs an answer..."

On August 26, Secretary of the Treasury, Henry Morgenthau Jr., the only Jew in Roosevelt's cabinet, received a letter from Peter which reminded him that there had recently been an agency created to save European monuments, and yet there was no such governmental group to save four million European Jews who were about to be slaughtered. Yet many officials in the government were annoyed by Morgenthau's interest in the Jewish refugees, and in private referred to him as "that damned Jew in the Treasury Department."

Henry Morgenthau Jr., (standing) and Franklin D. Roosevelt, 1932.

Rabbis to the Rescue

Peter thought that if he could enlist some rabbis in his cause, he might be more successful in his efforts. Therefore, he invited leaders of the Union of Orthodox Rabbis of the United States and Canada to join him in a large march in Washington.

Peter's invitation was accepted, and so two days before Yom Kippur, October 6, 1943, over five hundred traditional

Rabbis converge in Washington DC on October 6, 1943. President Roosevelt did not meet with them.

rabbis marched in Washington from Union Station, a major train station and transportation hub, to the Capitol. Their message: Save European Jews!

The rabbis spoke to radio and newsreel reporters, insisting that the U.S. government create a special agency to rescue the remnant of Israel.

President Roosevelt was angered by the march and refused to meet with the rabbis. In fact, the president's chief Jewish aide, Judge Samuel Rosenman, warned the president that the traditional, black-coated rabbis were "not your kind of Jews." Rosenman informed Zionist leaders that the president was very displeased by the march which Peter had organized.

Despite the negative attitude of Roosevelt and the major Zionist groups, led by Reform rabbis (Wise, Silver and others), many important American newspapers, such as the papers owned by Hearst, demonstrated strong support for a special agency.

One of the facts not well known to the general public is that the major Jewish organizations did everything possible to blacken the name of Peter Bergson and prevent him from accomplishing his main goal: the saving of Jewish lives. This is a very dark mark in the history of American Jewry.

Today, the American Jewish Committee is one of the most important and helpful Jewish organizations that exists. Fortunately, it has matured and awakened to the actual needs of American Jewry. But during the years of the *Shoah* (Holocaust) it was a different organization. The AJC sent letters to anyone asking about the Bergsonites.

Their letter stated:

"The efforts which these people proposed to make for the

rescue of Jews cannot be a duplication of efforts already made and being made by organizations which are recognized as representing the Jewish community of America."

History and facts show that it was only the Bergsonites who were advocating for a rescue agency. The mainstream groups were, sadly, openly antagonistic to the goals of the Bergson group.

One of the most distinguished Christian theologians of the twentieth century was Prof. Reinhold Niebuhr. As professor at Union Theological Seminary for over three decades, Niebuhr became a leading public intellectual and received the Presidential Medal of Freedom in 1964. TIME magazine called him "the greatest Protestant theologian in America."

As a supporter of the Bergson group, Professor Niebuhr understood the jealousy of those who opposed them, since the Bergsonites were focused on activities to rescue Jews, which those people in the opposition wished they could also be doing.

The Rumania Fiasco

During the winter of 1942-43, the government of Rumania offered to "sell" Jews.

Rumanian dictator Ion Antonescu made an offer to world Jewish organizations to receive $130 per person for allowing 70,000 Jews to be sent to any refuge location designated by the allies.

The Bergsonites saw this as a great opportunity. Ben Hecht wrote the copy for a very large advertisement in *The New York Times* and other major newspapers under the heading, "FOR SALE to Humanity 70,000 Jews." Further it

---

FOR SALE to Humanity
70,000 Jews
Guaranteed Human Beings at $50 a Piece

---

stated: "The Doors of Rumania Are Open. Act Now!"

Immediately Rabbi Wise issued a statement condemning the ad and the Bergsonites, claiming that there had been no "official" confirmation of the facts, and naming the whole thing a hoax. Peter was amazed at this reaction since Adolph Berle, a State Department official, confirmed the Rumanian offer. Unfortunately, the reaction of Rabbi Wise put a strong damper on the project. In his autobiography Rabbi Wise wrote: "The honor of Israel, the values of civilization, the ideals of mankind are even more precious than life itself."

This failure to save Jewish lives is one of the most disgraceful events of the entire battle between Peter Bergson and Rabbi Wise. Instead of shouting from the rooftops, Rabbi Wise let a golden opportunity disappear. Wise and his associates appeared to be spending more of their energy denouncing Bergson than supporting Zionism.

In a letter to a State Department aide, one of Wise's associates wrote:

"Everything must be done to liquidate the Bergsonites."

Rabbi Wise tried to have Peter deported since he was not an American citizen. One of Wise's associates stated that Rabbi Wise "regarded Bergson equally as great an enemy of the Jews as Hitler." They were so obsessed with Peter that they sent letters to every ambassador in Washington warning them that the Bergsonites did not represent the Jewish people, and were nothing but swindlers. On December 30, 1943, Rabbi Wise met with Congressman Sol Bloom of Manhattan, and told him that the Bergson group's efforts were part of an "evil and wretched plot."

Peter Bergson was a strong leader, and had one and only one goal in mind – rescuing Jewish lives. He refused to let his obsessed opponents restrain him. Finally, he was able to push through one plan that helped his fellow Jews.

Hope for The War Refugee Board

From the moment Peter learned of Hitler's "Final Solution," he knew that there was only one goal for which he would spend every hour of every day: the rescue of Jewish lives.

After many months of overcoming obstacles, such as the U.S. State Department, the major Zionist organizations, and a few Jewish leaders with huge egos that did not permit them to see beyond their own personal needs, Peter worked to promote one idea: the creation of an independent government agency, not connected to the State Department, to enable European Jews who were able to escape the Nazis.

When the pressure on President Roosevelt became too strong to avoid, and such an agency came into being, it was the Bergsonites most important accomplishment. Ironically, the major Jewish organizations which were trying to prevent this agency from coming into being, tried to demand all the credit.

Peter knew that the first step in getting a resolution passed in Congress was to persuade his congressional allies to present the idea to their colleagues. On November 9, 1943, Resolution 203 was introduced by three members of Congress who were close to Peter: Senator Guy Gillette of

Iowa, Senator Elbert Thomas of Utah, and Senator Edwin Johnson of Colorado.

The resolution stated:

"Congress recommends and urges the creation by the President of a commission of diplomatic, economic and military experts to formulate a plan of immediate action designed to save the surviving Jewish people of Europe from extinction at the hands of Nazi Germany."

It was only through the force of the American government that anything could be done to save the lives of European Jewry.

The same day, similar resolutions were presented in the House of Representatives, Resolutions 350 and 352, by Representative Will Rogers, Jr., and Representative Joseph C. Baldwin.

The Rescue Resolution was presented to the public at a news conference by the Emergency Committee. They explained that the first priority of such a new agency would be to establish transit camps in neutral countries, such as Turkey, Spain, Switzerland and Sweden. At some later point the refugees could be moved to Palestine.

Meanwhile, Peter had Ben Hecht, who did most of the writing for the newspaper ads, draw up a powerful advertisement called "My Uncle Abraham Reports." The ad appeared in *The Washington Post, The New York Times* and other major papers during the period of November 5 to November 22. The ad attacked Stalin, Roosevelt and Churchill for not paying attention to the life-and-death issues of the Jewish people. Hecht creatively made up a person called "Uncle Abraham," whose ghost, he suggested, would haunt Roosevelt for ignoring the Jewish problem.

My Uncle Abraham Reports

By Ben Hecht

I have an uncle who is a Ghost.

But, he is no ordinary Ghost like so many dead uncles.

He was elected last April by the Two Million Jews who have been murdered by the Germans to be their World Delegate.

Wherever there are conferences on how to make the World a Better Place, maybe, my Uncle Abraham appears and sits on the window sill and takes notes.

That's how he happened to be in Moscow a few weeks ago.

My Uncle Abraham sat on the window sill of the Kremlin and listened with great excitement, to one of the Finest Conferences he has ever attended since he has been a World Delegate.

He heard every word that Eden, Molotov and Hull spoke.

Last night my Uncle Abraham was back in a Certain Place where the Two Million murdered Jews meet. It is the Jewish Underground. Only Ghosts belong to it.

When the Two Million Souls had assembled, my Uncle Abraham arose and made his report to them as World Delegate.

"Dishonored dead," said my Uncle Abraham, "Fellow Corpses, and Ghosts from All Over. Of the Moscow Conference I have this to report. The Conference made a promise that the world was going to punish the Germans for murdering all the different peoples of Europe – Czechs, Greeks, Serbs, Russians, French hostages, Polish officers, Cretan peasants. Only we were not mentioned. In this conference, which named everyone, only the Jew had no name. He had no face. He was like a hole in Europe on which nobody looked."

A Ghost from the Lime Kilns of Warsaw spoke.

"Why is this?" asked this Ghost, "why is it that we who are dead without a Name in the Conferences of Fine People?"

"This I do not know," said my Uncle Abraham, "I can only report what exists. Jews do not exist, even when they are dead. In the Kremlin in Moscow, in the White House in Washington. In the Downing Street Building in London where I have sat on the windows sills, I have never heard our name. The people who live in those buildings – Stalin, Roosevelt and Churchill – do not speak of us. Why, I don't know. We were not allowed by the Germans to stay alive. We are not allowed by the Four Freedoms to be dead."

A woman Ghost from the Dynamite Dumps of Odessa spoke.

"If they didn't mention the two million murdered Jews in the Conference, isn't that bad for four million who are still alive? The Germans will think that when they kill Jews, Stalin, Roosevelt and Churchill pretend nothing is happening."

And from the Two Million Ghosts came a great cry.

"Why is this silence? Why don't they speak of Us?"

My Uncle Abraham raised his hand.

"Little Children," my Uncle Abraham spoke: "Be patient. We will be dead a long time. Yesterday when we were killed we were changed from Nobodies to No_bodies. Today, on our Jewish tomb, there is not the Star of David, there is an Asterisk. But, who knows, maybe Tomorrow – !"

This ended the Meeting of the Jewish Underground.

My Uncle Abraham has gone to the White House in Washington. He is sitting on the windowsill two feet away from Mr. Roosevelt. But he has left his notebook behind.

HELP PREVENT 4,000,000 PEOPLE FROM BECOMING GHOSTS, THERE ARE 4,000,000 JEWS STILL ALIVE IN EUROPE.

They can be saved ... We need your financial help immediately. By your support will be determined the speed, scope and effectiveness of our work to save the Jewish people of Europe.

Emergency committee to Save the Jewish people of Europe. Co-Chairmen: Peter H. Bergson, Louis Bromfield, Dr. Max Lerner, Ben Hecht, Rep. Will Rogers, Jr., and Mme. Sigrid Undset.

Published as a paid advertisement in *The New York Times*, Friday November 5, 1943.

President Roosevelt was greatly annoyed by these ads, though it apparently was enough to force the issue. Only one day after the news conference, on November 10, 1943, Roosevelt invited Undersecretary of State Edward Stettinius to discuss what could be done for the Jews, including the possibility of the agency which Peter wanted. Finally, President Roosevelt was doing something – probably under pressure of the huge publicity being aimed at his failure to act.

Predictably, both the State Department and the leading Jewish organizations opposed the resolution. Nevertheless, the resolution passed the Senate unanimously (Peter's friends wisely chose a day when one of his opponents was not present).

Passing the resolution in the Senate was crucial, but next it also had to pass in the House of Representatives. To pass in the House, the resolution had to be discussed in the Foreign Relations Committee, where the chairman, Sol Bloom, was opposed to anything that Peter wanted to do.

Bergson (L) with Congressman Andrew Somers. In 1942, Somers submitted a resolution in the House of Representatives calling on President Roosevelt to petition Great Britain "to take such action as may be necessary to permit the organization of all-Jewish military units in Palestine".

The Committee hearings on the bill began on November 19, 1943, and concluded December 2.

Congressman Bloom and Peter Bergson argued back and forth for days. Peter was relentless in his effort to promote the resolution, and every time Congressman Bloom challenged him, he replied strongly and brought the discussion back to the matter of saving Jewish lives.

Finally, Peter repeated his main theme for Bloom and the committee.

"The passage of the resolution is at the present moment the reason for the existence of my Emergency Committee. We

exist in order to save the Jews of Europe. Today the biggest thing that is being done in which the Jews of Europe can have some hope is this resolution."

The representatives of the major Zionist organizations were careful not to oppose the idea of saving Jewish lives. So, their attack on Peter's resolution was that it did not include any mention of Palestine, or Zionism.

They went back and forth, with Congressman Bloom trying to delay passage of the resolution as long as possible, and if he could, to defeat it.

To help break up the log jam, Representative Will Rogers, Jr. said that he doubted the advisability of bringing in the question of Palestine, since the resolution was specifically directed toward rescue. He explained that the Bergson group members were at least as committed as Rabbi Wise to see an independent national Jewish home in Palestine, but at this crucial hour, when the lives of millions of Jews are at stake, it would be foolhardy to hold up the important rescue matter.

Rogers kept harping on his main theme – getting the Jews out is our central question. Where they go is a different question, and not the purview of this committee right now.

After much hard work and lobbying Congress and others, Peter finally achieved his most important goal.

Success

Peter knew from the start that getting his resolution for the "rescue" of European Jews would be an uphill battle. He may not have realized the many hurdles and obstacles he would have to overcome.

In January 1944, the magazine *Congress Weekly*, overseen by Rabbi Wise, who headed the American Jewish Congress (AJC), criticized the Bergsonites for their requests for support from the Christian community.

The article in the magazine argued that "Any fly-by-night organization composed of a few energetic individuals can persuade these good people to give their names to the cause of saving the Jewish millions of Europe from extermination."

Soon after Wise's American Jewish Conference again attacked the Bergson group as "opportunists" representing an insignificant political party "whose only purpose was to spread chaos and demoralization in Jewish life."

Peter thought that perhaps if he approached the president of the AJC, Judge Joseph M. Proskauer, he could possibly change his mind. In a letter to the judge, Peter wrote:

"We must keep before us just one grim fact – we must

rescue Jews who are about to die. If they are allowed to die, their blood will be on our hands, for there can be no greater sin against God or man than to permit divergence of opinion on internal political questions among Jewish American groups that affect the rescue of millions of Jews in Europe."

In his battle to achieve his goal of the creation of a governmental agency independent of the State Department, Peter had both critics and supporters. Among his supporters were a few expressions from Jewish groups.

Rabbi Eliezer Silver, president of the American Union of Orthodox Rabbis, strongly objected to the vilification of the Bergsonites by Reform rabbinical organizations, claiming that such defamation is contrary to Jewish law.

In addition, Peter received support from one liberal stream of Judaism. On January 21, 1944, *The Reconstructionist* magazine claimed that the Bergsonites "filled a vacuum created by many years of ineffective activity on the part of Zionist bodies and philanthropic organizations."

A third source of support for Peter was Rabbi Meir Berlin, head of the most important Zionist religious party, World Mizrachi. Rabbi Berlin complained that the leaders of several organizations blocked the Bergsonites' significant efforts to arouse Americans to the importance of rescue. It was a matter of *pikuah nefesh*, saving lives. After Rabbi Berlin returned to Palestine from his trip in the U.S., he called a press conference in Jerusalem in June 1944, castigating those who tried to block the resolution.

Fortunately, several members of the Department of the Treasury were sympathetic to the idea of preserving lives in the face of Hitler's "Final Solution." One argument that was presented to President Roosevelt that he could identify with, was that if Congress did not pass this resolution, it would look bad for the President from a political point of view.

On January 16, 1944, Secretary of the Treasury, Henry Morgenthau, Jr., along with a few of his aides, made an appointment with Roosevelt with a "Personal Report to the President." The report listed the "utter failure" of State Department officials to assist the Jews of Europe.

The President, who wanted to beat the Bergsonites to the punch, signed Executive Order No. 9417, establishing a presidential agency for saving Jews, officially called the War Refugee Board.

The special agency was ordered to "take all measures within its power to rescue the victims of enemy oppression." This included developing plans and taking measures for the rescue, transportation, maintenance and relief of the victims of the Nazis, and to establish "havens of temporary refuge" for them. In order to achieve these goals, the various departments of government including Departments of State, War and Treasury, were directed to carry out all requests of the War Refugee Board.

It was clear that Roosevelt's positive action, in contrast to his previous total lack of interest in saving Jewish lives, was in large measure in reaction to the work of Peter Bergson and his group. On January 24, 1944, the *Christian Science Monitor* wrote that Roosevelt's decision to create the WRB "is the outcome of pressure brought to bear by the Emergency Committee to Save the Jewish People of Europe, a group made up of both Jews and non-Jews that has been active in the capital in recent month."

In addition, the editor of the *New York Post* wrote to Peter to praise his work: "I think your activities in the country for the past two years have resulted in the one effective step taken thus far to break through the dyke of indifference, intolerance, suspicion and opposition."

Further, the publisher of the Scripps-Howard newspaper chain said that his newspapers would continue to assist the Emergency Committee "not only because of admitted worthiness of your cause, but because of our belief that the methods you are apparently determined to employ are the most apt to be productive."

Wise's American Jewish Conference issued a press release congratulating the President for establishing the War Refugee Board (WRB). They claimed responsibility for its creation, that "the Conference's Commission of Rescue had asked the government to establish this interdepartmental board and representatives of the commission have been negotiating with government officials to that end for some time."

While Rabbi Wise was taking all this credit, Secretary Morgenthau gave credit to the Bergson group for getting "the President really to act on this – we are talking here among ourselves."

The Work of Raoul Wallenberg

The first director of the WRB was John Pehle, a bright young assistant at Treasury. One of the tasks of the Board was to join with envoys from neutral countries. Raoul Wallenberg of Sweden was one of them. Wallenberg was especially courageous, and was able to save tens of thousands of Jews in Hungary. With the help of the Board, Wallenberg, just 32 years old, a descendant of a well-known Swedish banking dynasty, was given the necessary diplomatic cover.

Raoul Wallenberg.

Wallenberg used documents – some of which were legal, and others forged. He also used bribery and other shady means to achieve his goals.

For many years the sacred work of Wallenberg was not well-known or appreciated. Things changed in recent times, and his heroic efforts were finally recognized. It also became more known that it was the War Refugee Board that played a very important and historic role in his endeavors.

Since the work of the War Refugee Board served a humanitarian need, and not merely a Jewish need, the budget would naturally come from the U.S. government. Fearing that the perception of the government funding a cause to save Jews might provoke antisemitism, Peter encouraged Jewish organizations to provide the needed money. The Bergson group in general was disappointed that the government was not paying for this budget, considering it a harmful restriction on the WRB. This hampered the scope of activities of the Board, and detracted from its importance in the public's eyes. The President had a fund of 50 million dollars at his disposal, which he decided not to use.

Nevertheless, even though the Board had a small staff of thirty workers, it was successful in saving thousands of Jewish lives. Hundreds of Jews in Greece were sent to neutral Spain, and not to the death camp at Auschwitz. Thousands of other Jews were saved in the Balkans, in southeast Europe.

Jewish lives were saved, according to official records of the WRB in several ways. "Lesser German officials were bribed. False identification papers were supplied. Border officials were bribed to pass refugees. Tens of thousands were rescued from Nazi extermination by these clandestine means."

These events of rescue proved that it might have been possible to save many thousands, perhaps hundreds of thousands, had the State Department and Zionist leaders not for such a long time ignored the pleas of the Bergson group, and blocked suggestions of others.

Soon after the creation of the War Refugee Board, Peter had many prominent ads placed in several newspapers, urging Great Britain to open the gates to Palestine, and put an end to the unfair White Paper which limited Jewish immigration to the Promised Land. The ads quoted the Archbishop of Canterbury who called for the saving of Jewish lives. "We all stand before the bar of history, of humanity and of God," he said.

When the War Refugee Board wrote its Final Summary Report in May 1945, over 50,000 Jews had been ransomed. Altogether, historians credit the agency with saving about 200,000 lives.

Sadly, had the WRB been created earlier, many more lives could have been saved. It was too little, too late.

The Next Step

After Peter and his colleagues had succeeded in creating an agency to help save Jewish lives, the War Refugee Board, he began to think about what next steps he and his group should take.

Peter and his group decided to launch "The Hebrew Committee of National Liberation." It was officially announced in Washington on May 18, 1944.

The aims of the group were to continue promoting new ideas to help the surviving Jews in Europe; and to create a dramatic public campaign to undo the British restrictions on immigration to Eretz Yisrael.

One of Peter's ideas was to bring Jewish refugees to America, which prided itself on being "the haven of the oppressed." Unfortunately, President Roosevelt and his State Department very much disliked the notion of bringing rescued Jews to the United States for the rest of the war.

While not happy with this idea, the President finally relented in June 1944. He established the Emergency Refugee Shelter at Fort Ontario, in Oswego, in upstate New York. Thus, one thousand stateless Jews, fleeing Germany, Austria, the Balkans and Southern Italy, were brought to the United States. This special arrangement was outside the quota of American immigration laws.

When the president advised Congress of his action, he insisted that these one thousand Jews would be held under "appropriate security restrictions until they could be returned to their homelands" after the war.

When the refugees arrived, they thanked the President and the WRB, and the Bergson group. In a telegram to the Bergsonites, they wrote:

"God be with you. Blessed be those who assist you in your holy work for the salvation of the remnants of Israel."

Had this idea of an Emergency Refugee Shelter been multiplied, many more Jewish lives could have been saved. Alas, it turned out to be only a token gesture, with Roosevelt hoping that this one act of compassion would stifle further criticism of the White House. When asked about repeating this idea, Roosevelt said "We do not need any more free ports at the present time." His one-time action turned out to be a highly publicized, but superficial move.

While Peter continued to press for more such Refugee Shelters, his efforts were to no avail. Nevertheless, by forcing the President to create the WRB and one Emergency Refugee Shelter, Peter did more than anyone else to try to save Jewish lives.

Almost all of the mainstream Zionists continued their attacks on the Bergson group. It is a black mark on the nations of the world, including the United States, and American Jewry, that so many of our people perished when many could have been saved.

One significant Zionist stood by Peter, to his great credit.

Gershon Agronsky, the American-born journalist, who was the founding editor of *The Palestine Post* (after 1948 renamed *The Jerusalem Post*), and later mayor of Jerusalem, attempted to publish an editorial criticizing Peter's opponents. Unfortunately, the British censors refused to permit publication of his editorial.

The editorial is significant because it recognizes Peter's special contribution to Jewish history.

Agronsky's editorial reads as follows:

Throughout the war years Peter Bergson played an important national role in the United States. Backed by no official authority, and thanks only to his energy, application, natural talent and faith, he succeeded in drawing the attention of extensive circles in the United States to our problem. He was the first to conduct propaganda on a large scale hitherto unknown to Jewish endeavor anywhere in the world for the creation of a Jewish Army to make war on the Nazi regime. He succeeded in attracting many friends to this idea not only in America but also in Britain. The creation of the Jewish Brigade [a few months before the war ended] owes much to his efforts. He was the first to try to influence the U.S. Government to tackle the question of Jewish refugees, and was the man who broke down the wall of silence that surrounded the annihilation of the Jews of Europe. He was the first to bring to the fore in the United States the question of representation of the Hebrew nation in international deliberations and showed the way to activity in this direction. With his political sense and his dynamic personality which impressed all those who came into contact with him – Jews as well as gentiles – he knew how to overcome the many difficulties that beset him in his work. The Jewish People is very poor in forces endowed with the courage to stand guard over its interests. It would indeed be a pity if for formal reasons, Peter Bergson's work in the United States should at this decisive hour cease.

Summing Up

Chaim Weizmann, the Russian-born biochemist and Zionist leader who later became the first president of the State of Israel, serving from February 1949 until his death in November 1952, delivered a prophetic speech at Madison Square Garden on March 1, 1943.

Chaim Weizmann.

Here are Weizmann's prophetic words:

"When the Historian of the future assembles the bleak record of our days, he will find two things unbelievable: first, the crime itself; second, the reaction of the world to that crime."

While the American government and the major Jewish organizations did precious little to prevent the massacre of six million Jews, Peter Bergson/Hillel Kook stands out as a bright light in his remarkable efforts to save as many Jewish lives as he could.

For that he will go down in history as one of the great heroes of the Jewish people.

Bibliography

Baumel, Judith Tydor. *The "Bergson Boys" and the Origins of Contemporary Zionist Militancy* (Syracuse, New York: Syracuse University Press, 2005).

Medoff, Rafael. *The Jews Should Keep Quiet: Franklin D. Roosevelt, Rabbi Stephen S. Wise and the Holocaust.* (Philadelphia: Jewish Publication Society, 2019).

Medoff, Rafael and Golinkin, David. *The Student Struggle Against the Holocaust.* (Jerusalem: Schechter Institute for Jewish Studies, 2010).

Rapoport, Louis. *Shake Heaven and Earth: Peter Bergson and the Struggle to Rescue the Jews of Europe.* (Jerusalem: Gefen Publishing House, 1999).

Wyman, David S. *The Abandonment of the Jews: America and the Holocaust, 1941-1945.* (New York: The New Press, 1984).

Wyman, David S. and Rafael Medoff. *A Race Against Death: Peter Bergson, America and the Holocaust.* (New York: The New Press, 2002).

Made in the USA
Middletown, DE
14 September 2022

10421494R00050